Convert your Minivan into a Mini RV Camper

How to convert a minivan into a comfortable minivan camper motorhome

William H. Myers

www.bmyers.com

Version 2016.03.01

ISBN-13: 978-1530265121
ISBN-10: 1530265126

Contents

Introduction

In this book you'll learn how to convert almost any minivan into a comfortable mini RV camper, perfect for short or long term camping.

You won't need any special tools, won't have to buy lumber or use a saw or power tools, and won't need to drill holes or make any permanent changes to your minivan.

If you follow the steps shown in this book, you'll end up with a minivan camper that has:

- a comfortable bed

- a toilet

- a small kitchen

- plenty of storage cabinets

- back up power supply

- fan and heater

- TV

- small fridge and cooler

- privacy curtains

- awning or sun shade

- and more

You'll have everything you need to stealth camp just about anywhere in the world. All you'll need to add is your clothes and food.

You'll be able to install everything in less than an hour, and convert your mini camper back into a stock van in just a few minutes.

In each chapter you'll find photos and sources for every item mentioned. I won't waste your time with unnecessary writing and will show you the quick and easy way to convert your minivan into a comfortable camper.

One last point – everything I show here will also work in larger vans so if you at some point decide to upgrade to a full sized cargo or conversion van, you'll be able to use everything shown in this book.

That said, let's get started.

Why a minivan?

I've owned a number a motorhomes, ranging from the very large class A diesel pushers, to mid size Class C's, to the smaller cargo van Class B's.

I've camped and criss-crossed the country in these full size motorhomes many times. At the end of each trip, I invariably sold the motorhome and looked for something smaller, easier to drive with better fuel mileage and a higher stealth factor.

My most recent motorhome was a small Roadtrek 170, and it was almost the perfect size. Small enough to park just about anywhere with fairly decent fuel economy.

It had a bath with toilet, a shower, a kitchen with fridge and microwave, a TV and a full bed in the back. Underneath, it had a generator to provide electrical power when not hooked up to an external power source.

Like I said, it was almost perfect. But it was expensive. A new Roadtrek like the one I had would cost close to a hundred thousand dollars. Even ten year old used ones cost thirty five thousand or more.

For all that money, what you are really getting is a truck based cargo van packed with expensive appliances, a toilet and sewage holding tank.

Being a cargo van, these small Class B's often ride and handle like overloaded work trucks. They wallow in the wind, suck down fuel and are way too expensive to risk taking off road or parking in places where they could get damaged or broken into.

Still, they are great to camp in and offer the opportunity to travel at a moments notice and camp just about anywhere with most of the comforts of home.

But I wanted more. I wanted to be able to camp in something less expensive, something that handled better, used less fuel and was much more stealthy.

That's why I decided to sell my Roadtrek, get a minivan and convert it to a motorhome that would have almost everything the Roadtrek had in it.

There are many advantages of a minivan, and they include:

1. **They are easy to drive, easy to park, and very maneuverable.** Whether on the highway cruising along at seventy or poking around town they are up to the task. They do well in all sorts of weather, are packed with all kinds of modern automotive amenities and have lots of space inside.

2. **They are affordable** – minivans have been around since the mid 1980's and there are literally millions of them on the road. You can find them on almost every used car lot, with prices starting just over a thousand dollars. Even late model, highly reliable and well configured ones can be found for under six thousand dollars.

3. **They have a lot of room inside** – remove the back two rows of seats from a minivan and you have more cargo space than in most full size pickup trucks. Almost all minivans have room for a 4' x 8' sheet of plywood with a foot or two to spare.

4. **They are multi use vehicles** – a minivan can be your daily driver, can be used to haul your kids, your pets, furniture, and just about anything else that you can fit inside the rear and side doors. I've seen people haul goats in them.

5. **Minivans are safe** – modern minivans are designed so occupants can survive a crash. They are packed with safety features, everything from eight to ten airbags, backup monitors, adaptive cruise control, parental lockout, crush zones and more. Crash tests have shown that modern minivans are safer in a crash than full size trucks or SUVs.

6. **They have a great stealth factor** – You can park a minivan just about anywhere and it won't draw attention or suspicion. This is important if you are boondocking in a Walmart parking lot or curb camping in places like Key West or San Francisco.

7. **You can use it every day** – after you've converted your minivan to a camper, you can still use it as your daily driver. No need to take the camping gear out. No one will know the difference. Should you decide to take a nap, make a meal, watch a little TV, you can do in it your minivan-camper and no one will notice.

8. **It won't sit unused** - If you had one of those big motorhomes, it would most likely sit in your driveway or storage lot, unused most of the year. It's too big and expensive to use as a daily driver and difficult to park. With a minivan camper, you can use it every day.

As you can see, there are many good reasons to choose a minivan as a basis for your mini-RV camper. But, there are also **some disadvantages**.

These include:

1. **Limited interior space** – there is a reason they are called 'mini vans'. They have less interior space than full size vans.

2. **Limited headroom** – most minivans will have a floor to ceiling height of four feet or less. This means you won't be able to stand up inside and will be crouched over or on your knees as you move around inside the camper conversion. This is the biggest negative of a minivan camper, but one most people get used to fairly quickly.

3. **Limited 'Cool' factor** – motorhome and RV owners are going to look down on those who camp in minivans, especially if you're camping in an RV park. People who have invested fifty to several hundred thousand dollars in a 'real' motorhome are not going to be impressed with your minivan camper.

Minivan camping is not for everyone. If you need room to stand up inside the van, or if you need space for more than two people to sleep, or if the 'cool' factor is important to you, a minivan is probably not the right camper for you.

But if you want a low profile stealthy camper that can go just about anywhere with most of the comforts of home at a fraction of the cost of a full size motorhome, converting a minivan into a mini-RV camper might be just the ticket.

In the following chapters, I'll show you how to do it.

Choosing the right minivan

When it comes to choosing the right minivan to convert to a mini-RV, you have many different makes and models to choose from.

To make the process easier, here's what to look for.

1. **Removable or fold down, fold flat seats** – make sure the minivan you are considering has either completely removable rear seats or seats that fold flat into the floor. If the two rows of rear seats can't be removed or folded flat into the floor, find another van.

2. **Removable center console** – if there's a center console between the front driver and passenger seats, make sure it is removable. You'll want the space between the front seats clear, so you can crawl to the back of the van from the front without going outside.

3. **Maximum interior height** – measure the distance between the floor and the ceiling inside the middle of the back of the van. As a minimum you'll want thirty six inches. More is better.

4. **Maximum interior width** – measure the distance between the walls in the back. As a minimum you'll want forty eight inches wide. More is better.

5. **Presentable outside appearance** – if you'll be stealth camping in your minivan, you'll want it to look

reasonably new, clean and dent free. Avoid vans that have been repainted, have rust or major dents. You don't want people calling the police when they see your minivan parked in their neighborhood, so get one that looks presentable.

6. **Good mechanical condition** – As with any vehicle you plan to drive, you want it to have good brakes, tight steering, reliable engine and transmission, quiet muffler and be in overall good condition. With the hundreds of thousands of used minivans on the market, there's no reason not to get one that isn't in excellent condition inside and out.

My personal choice

I've owned a number of minivans and when it comes to which one I'd buy for converting to a mini-RV, the choice, at least for me, is clear. The model I like and own is the Toyota Sienna.

I chose the Sienna for a number of reasons. Like all Toyotas, they are reliable, safe and easy to drive. They are packed with safety features, are available with dual electric doors and have more interior space than most other minivans.

Of the various Sienna models, the second gen Sienna's (2004 – 2010) are the easiest to convert and offer the most value for the dollar – especially the LE models – which are a step above the base van.

Third gen Sienna's (2011 and newer), have a few more features but not all models have a customer removable front console or totally removable middle row seats. These vans can still be converted into mini-RVs but require a bit more work.

I know this to be true because I currently own a 3rd gen Sienna, and as you'll see in some of photos in this book, the middle seat rails remain in floor after the seats have been removed.

My previous Sienna was a 2006 and the back seats could be removed leaving a flat floor, making for a good starting point for a mini-RV conversion

3ʳᵈ Generation Toyota Sienna

Obviously, there are other good minivan choices, including the Honda Odyssey, Dodge Caravan, Chrysler Town and Country, and KIA Sedona.

As long as the van you are considering is in good condition, has removable seats and removable front console, it'll work for a camper conversion.

Just make sure the open space behind the front seats is as least six feet – more is better.

Getting started with a minivan camper conversion

The first step to converting your minivan to a mini-RV camper is to remove the middle and back row seats.

In most cases, the middle row seats can be removed by pulling a lower handle and lifting the seat out.

However, these seats can weigh forty pounds or more and you might need help getting them out. So before you try to remove the seats for the first time, look in the vehicle's owners manual for the steps needed to remove them.

Before removing the seats, figure out where you are going to store them. You won't want to leave them outside to be damaged by rain or sun, because some day you'll probably want to put them back in.

In my van, the middle row seats weighed about sixty pounds each and were cumbersome to carry. To make it easier, I used a two-wheel dolly to move the seats into our garage for storage.

Seat removed – it was heavy!

After removing and storing the middle row seats, the next step is to either remove or fold flat the rear row of seats. As before, review your owner's manual to see how it is done.

In my van, the seats folded flat into the floor.

Back row seats need to be folded flat or removed

After removing the middle and back row of seats, you should have a fairly flat open surface.

Flat floor after seats are removed

A Little House Cleaning

After you remove the seats don't be surprised if you find a lot of junk left behind by the previous or current owners of the van. In my case, I found candy, nuts, pencils, tiny plastic toys, french fries and dried soda pop.

Finding these kinds of things in a used minivan is not unusual. Minivans are usually owned by families with kids, and in the process of hauling them around, their droppings fall under the seats and eventually find their way into the vans cracks and crevices.

Knowing that, when you get the seats out, take the time to give your minivan a good cleaning. Start by vacuuming the carpet and cleaning all the hidden cubby holes and storage bins. You may even want to go the extra step of cleaning the carpet.

Keep in mind you'll be camping and sleeping in the van and you probably don't want to live with the smells and debris left by the previous owner(s).

After you vacuum the van out, get a sponge, a bucket of water and house hold cleaner, and clean all the plastic surfaces.

Take some time to get it clean!

After you get the inside walls and carpet cleaned, the next step is to clean the inside of the windows. You'll want to do this before you start the camper conversion.

After you clean the windows, go to the next chapter.

Window Treatment

With the two rows of rear seats removed and the interior cleaned and vacuumed, it's time to start working on the window treatments.

Since you'll be sleeping and maybe even living in your mini van, you'll want to take steps to give you some privacy while inside. You'll want to insulate the window glass so the van doesn't gain too much heat from the sun or lose it at night.

The easy solution for both privacy and insulation is to purchase a 24 inch wide by 25 foot long roll of Reflectix insulation. You can find it at Lowes, Home Depot, Ace Hardware and other home improvement stores as well as at Amazon online.

Reflectix is basically two layers of bubble wrap, bonded to an outer layer of highly reflective plastic. It is light weight, easy-to-cut with scissors and an ideal material to create sun block, privacy and insulation for your van's windows.

The reflective properties of Reflectix help keep the outside heat from coming into your van, and assist in maintaining the interior temperature at night.

Reflectix is waterproof, won't burn, has no smell and is easy to clean with a wet cloth. For most minivans, a 24 inch by 25 foot roll will be enough to cover all the windows except the windshield.

Roll of 24" x 25' Reflectix from Lowes

After you get your roll of Reflectix ($24 at Lowes), you'll want to unroll a small section and start cutting pieces to fit each of the windows in your van.

The easy way to do this is to measure the maximum length of a window and then using scissors, cut a piece of Reflectix about two inches longer than the measurement.

Unroll the Reflectix

Take the piece of Reflectix and press in into the window, folding the edges as needed to get a tight fit. Crease the edges well because you'll be using the creases as a pattern to trim for a better fit.

Remove the Reflectix from the window and use scissors to cut outside the crease lines by about ½ inch. Cutting the piece slightly larger than necessary will make it easier to keep the Reflectix in the window without needing anything to hold it in.

Press Reflectix into window to create cut pattern

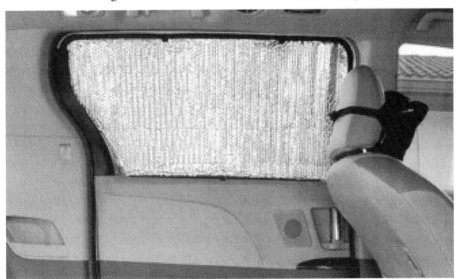

Trimmed to perfect fit

Repeat the process for all the windows, including the back window. Make sure the pieces fit tightly in each window so that light doesn't leak out.

You could cut a piece of Reflectix for the windshield, but you may find a custom fit sun shade to be a better solution. These store bought shades will have sewn edges and fit the window perfectly. You can find them at your local big box stores in the automotive section as well as at Amazon and http://www.autoanything.com/.

After you've cut and placed Reflectix on your windows, stand outside your van to see how it looks. If your van has tinted windows, the Reflectix should be almost invisible, especially after dark.

Reflectix almost invisible behind tinted windows

If the windows in your van aren't tinted and you want stealth, you may want to paint the outside of each piece of Reflectix, using a roller and black paint safe for plastic.

If you do decide to paint the pieces, only paint the outside of each piece. Doing so will let you flip the piece over and use the reflective side on hot sunny days.

If you don't paint the Reflectix and plan on keeping your van for a long time, it's a good idea to get the windows tinted. This will make the van more comfortable on sunny days and give another level of privacy and stealth when you camp.

Reflectix provides privacy and insulation

In addition to the Reflectix, you will also want a privacy curtain behind the driver and passenger seats. This will be useful when parking where putting Reflectix on the driver and passenger windows might appear suspicious.

You can leave those front windows uncovered and put the privacy curtain directly behind the front seats along with Reflectix in the back windows, and it'll look like your typical minivan with deep tinted side and back windows.

For this to work, choose a dark blue or black thermal

curtain. For my van, I found a 6' x 4' thermal curtain panel at Walmart for $9.84.

I used metal shower curtain rings to attach each end of the curtain to the driver and passenger grab handles at the top of the two front doors.

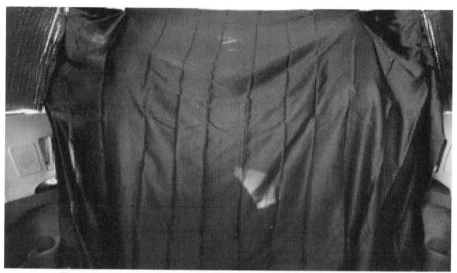

Privacy curtain across the back of front seats

Ventilation and Air Flow

Because you will be spending a lot of time inside your van you'll want a way to have air flow and ventilation, regardless of the weather.

You might be thinking, "I can just roll down the windows for ventilation." And in some cases, that'll work.

But if it's raining or if you are curb camping or boondocking, it might not be safe or practical to roll the windows down. Rain can get in, or worse, someone could break in.

A better solution is to install vent visors over all the windows that roll down. Vent visors cover the top two inches of the window, keeping rain and would-be robbers out, while letting fresh air in and giving humidity and heat a way to escape.

Vent visors are available for almost all mini vans, are easy to install and affordable. There are several brands available, but I find the AVS brand external vent visor to be the most affordable, while still being quite durable and requiring no tools to install.

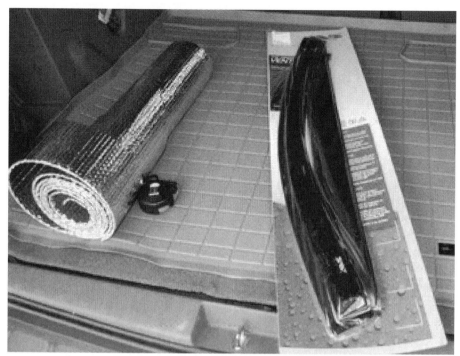

Package of four AVS vent visors

When it comes to choosing vent visors, you usually have a choice of 'in-channel' or 'external mount' visors.

The 'In-channel' visors fit inside the top of the window channel and are squeezed into the channel when you roll your window up.

The advantage of 'in-channel' is no taping is involved. However, some people experience increased wind noise with 'in-channel' visors.

The external mount visors are mounted by taping the visor to the door frame just above the window. The visors are delivered with the tape already attached and all you have to do is peel the skin off the tape and place the visor firmly on the door frame.

I've installed external visors on a number of vehicles and prefer them over the in channel ones.

External mount vent visor on Toyota Sienna

Having window vent visors means you can keep your windows rolled down an inch or more when parked or camping without worrying about rain or giving thieves easy access.

They can be ordered from Amazon and other places. I ordered custom fit ones for my Toyota Sienna from www.autoanything.com

One thing to note – when camping in areas with mosquitoes and other flying insects, you'll want to place bug screens in the open window gaps to keep the little monsters out. To do this, buy a small roll of thirty inch wide window screen material from Home Depot or Lowes, and cut small pieces to jam into the window openings when you camp.

The screens won't be visible from the outside and will keep the bugs from getting in.

Vent visors all around – looking good!

A comfortable bed

One of the most important things to have in your mini-RV camper is a comfortable bed. While there are many ways to add a bed to your minivan, the easiest and perhaps the most comfortable is to use a spring loaded camp cot.

Unlike other cots, a spring loaded cot has no support bars underneath the cot fabric that can dig into your back during the night. Like a trampoline, springs hold the cot material to the side frame which lets it flex and adjust for your weight.

For the single person traveling alone, a spring loaded folding camp cot is the ideal bed. Light weight and comfortable and wide enough for a back or side sleeper. To make it even more comfortable, add a memory foam topper.

When it comes to which spring loaded camping cot to get, I recommend the Coleman Ridgeline III Folding Camping Cot, available at Walmart online for around $50.00.

The Coleman Ridgeline cot includes a one inch thick mattress which adds to the cot's comfort.

Coleman spring loaded camping cot in van

While there are a number of other spring loaded cots, I like this one because the cot is thirteen inches tall. This is important because it means you can sit on the cot and not hit your head on the van's ceiling.

It also means you can store items under the cot as long as they are no taller than twelve inches - you'll see later why this is very important.

As mentioned before, the cot includes a one-inch mattress. A lot of people find this is all they need. But for more comfort, I purchased a twin size three-inch memory foam mattress pad which I cut down to fit the cot.

Cot with three inch memory foam mattress

In the above photo, I have placed the cot (which is 76 inches long) against the back of the driver's seat. Notice how much room (almost two feet) is open behind it. Also notice how much free space is under the cot and to the right of it. You'll see why this is important later on.

A big advantage of this particular cot is it can quickly be folded and stored away. If you find something big on your trip that you want to haul back home, you can fold the cot, put it against the side wall, and have plenty of storage room left.

If more than one person will be sleeping in the van, this cot probably isn't the way to go as it is too wide to put two of them side by side in the van.

For two people, you could use a Coleman Queen Airbed cot, which you can find on Amazon for around $100.

Coleman Queen Airbed cot – about $100

The Coleman Queen will fit in the back of most minivans and will have plenty of room for storage underneath. You can read about it at http://www.amzn.to/1RjwP74

Another option when there's two people sleeping in the van is to use a folding futon. During the day you can fold the futon into a couch and store supplies under it. At night, you fold it out into a bed for two.

A futon will be heavier than a cot but if there's two of you, it's better than sleeping on the floor.

When searching for the right futon, check local Goodwill and second hand shops, as often you can find great deals on used ones at those places. Look for futons without end arm rests to make them easier to use in the minivan.

If you do get a used futon, plan on throwing away the mattress and replacing it with one that no one else has slept on.

One last note – after you have your bed and all the other things in your minivan, you'll want to anchor them so they won't move during travel or during sudden stops. I use bungee cords connected to the numerous floor anchors to do this.

Toilet & bathroom

All full size RVs and motorhomes have a toilet and your minivan-RV should have one as well.

You might be thinking, "I'll just rely on bathrooms in rest areas, gas stations and fast food joints. I don't need a toilet in my minivan."

Maybe that'll work for you. But what if it doesn't?

What if while out on the road you suddenly need to use a toilet and the closest public rest room is miles away? What then?

Sure, you could pull over and find a tree, but depending on the weather, the geography, and the number of people around, that might not be the best idea.

A better idea is to have a toilet in your minivan. Something to handle number one as well as number two.

Even if you're not worried about bathroom emergencies while on the road, what about at night when you're trying to sleep? It's not going to be much fun if you have to get up and leave your van in the middle of the night to take a pee. Especially if it is cold or rainy or if you're camping on the street or near other campers.

Fortunately, there is an easy and affordable solution to having bathroom facilities in your minivan.

The first is a 'pee bottle' – these are what most truck and over the road drivers carry with them so they can relieve themselves without having to find a public restroom.

There are bottles designed for both men and women and most include a resealable cap as well as a handle. Not surprisingly, you can find them on sale at both <u>Amazon</u> and eBay (search for either 'Pee bottle' or 'urine bottle').

Bottles come in a variety of colors and sizes, and most are priced under $10.00.

Another option is to visit your local dollar store (IE Dollar Tree), and buy a plastic juice pitcher that has a handle and easy seal top. These can work just as well as pee bottles. Just be sure to label the pitcher so you know what's in it.

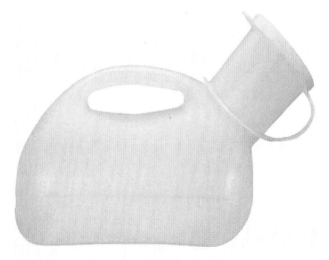

Male Pee bottle

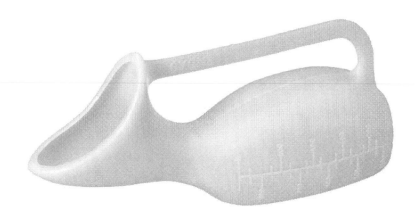

Female Pee bottle

In addition to the pee bottle(s), you'll want a small portable toilet for going 'number two'.

These are the kind of toilets used in smaller boats and older RVs. They look and operate like a regular toilet, except they are not connected to a sewer system. They have a built-in fresh water tank used to create a robust flush to send waste material into a lower and removable storage tank.

The lower tank is sealed to prevent spills and if used with tank deodorant chemicals, has no smell. When the lower tank needs to be emptied, you open two latches, remove the tank and take it to a dump station or bathroom to empty it.

Once the tank has been emptied, you connect it back to the toilet seat, refill the top tank with water, add the deodorant chemical and the toilet will be ready for another thirty to fifty uses.

Thetford and Dometic are the two most well known manufacturers of portable toilets and they offer them in several different heights and holding tank capacities. All are designed to handle the weight of a two hundred fifty pound adult.

The size toilet you choose should be based on the space you have available. In my minivan, I wanted a toilet that could be stored under the foot of the Coleman cot mentioned in an earlier chapter. That meant the toilet could be no more than twelve inches tall.

After doing some research, I found the Century 6205 2.6 Gallon Portable Toilet to be a perfect fit. <u>Amazon had it in stock</u> for $78.99. It's also available at Walmart and other stores for about the same price.

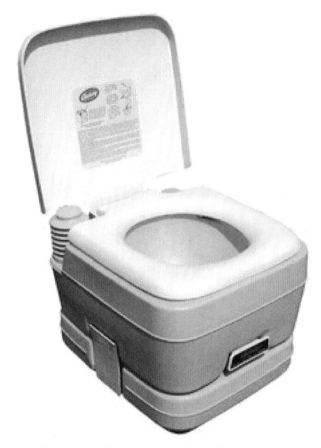

Century Portable 2.5 gallon toilet

The image below shows the toilet beside the Coleman cot in the minivan-RV.

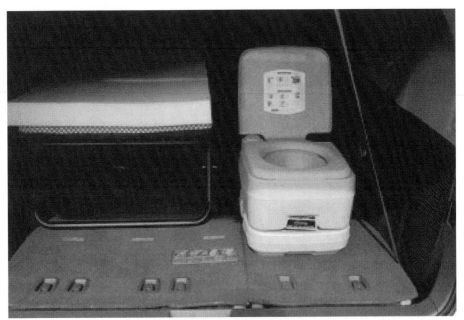

Toilet ready for use

Toilet fits under the Coleman cot

As you look at the above photo, notice how much room is left beside the portable toilet. That's where I store a small plastic milk crate with toilet paper, paper towels, hand wipes and the pee bottle mentioned earlier.

For washing hands, I carry a Coleman Party Stacker two gallon plastic jug with easy pour spigot. These jugs are eleven inches tall and can be stored under the cot.

Coleman Party Stacker 2 Water Cooler

When I need to wash, I place the water jug on top of the storage cabinet (see next chapter) with a plastic bucket below to catch excess water.

I carry two of them – a blue one for drinking and a red one for washing up. I found them on Walmart online for $10.94 each.

As with everything else you put in your van, you'll want to anchor these down so they don't move or spill during travel.

As a side note, I purchased many of the items mentioned in this book on Walmart's online site.

I use their free 'ship to store' feature to have the item shipped to the store and held for pickup.

Doing this allows me to purchase items from Walmart that are not normally stocked in their retail stores, and often for less than the price at Amazon and sometimes even lower than the price when the item is actually stocked in a Walmart store.

With the free ship-to store option, Walmart sends me an email when the item is available for pickup and I go to the store to get it.

Walmart online accepts PayPal payment in addition to all major credit cards.

Storage, storage, storage

When outfitting your minivan-RV, you'll want to have room for all the things you'll be carrying with you - clothes, food, cookware, cameras and computers.

If you use the Coleman cot that I showed in an earlier chapter, you'll have a lot of free space available for storage. To keep everything organized, I store almost everything in clear plastic totes and food containers that you can find at any big box store for a couple of dollars each.

When choosing containers, I always look for ones that are no taller than ten inches so that they fit under the cot. I also look for ones that are clear so I can see what's in them. On the larger tote, look for one with a flat top so it can double as a dinner table or a computer work station.

For clothes and tools, I use soft sided gym and tool bags. These bags expand to fit and are easily stored under the cot, behind the seats or up against walls.

Clear storage tub used for dry food storage

Soft bags for clothes, tools, cameras, computer

In addition to the plastic storage bins and soft-sided bags, I purchased two <u>Sterlite Three Drawer Storage Cabinets</u> from Walmart ($17.88 each), and placed them at the very back of the van.

Since the cot blocks the drawers on one of these, I turned it to face the outside of the van. The other one is not blocked, its drawer opens inside.

Two Sterlite three drawer storage cabinets

The three large drawers can be used to store cooking gear, tools, clothes, food and anything else you want to take with you.

The cabinets are made of plastic, are lightweight and easy to move in and out of the van. Being just twenty two inches tall they don't block the view out the back window.

With one cabinet facing forward and the other facing the back door, I can access three of the drawers inside the van and the other three when I open the back door. I keep the camp stove, pans and fuel in the back-facing cabinet, with heavy items in the bottom and lighter items in the top.

To secure the cabinets, I run a bungee cord from the wall anchors across the top front, which keeps them from tipping over.

Single Sterlite cabinet if you don't need two

If you need more storage than two of these cabinets provide, Walmart also has five drawer cabinets made of the same lightweight material. They are six inches taller and will partially block the view out the back window, so be careful if you choose to use them.

Personally, I prefer not blocking the view and I find two of the three-drawer cabinets along with the under bed storage more than sufficient for everything I carry with me when I camp.

Sterlite 5 drawer storage cabinet from Walmart

Cooking and Refrigeration

One of the big advantages of traveling in a minivan-RV is that unlike large RVs, you don't have to worry about whether there'll be enough room to pull into a grocery store parking lot or farmers market or small cafe. You won't have to wonder whether the RV is too tall to fit under the drive through or if the RV is over the parking lot's weight limit.

With a minivan-RV, you can pretty much fit anywhere. If you're traveling down the highway and see an interesting place to stop or pick up a meal, you can pull in without worries.

But what if you want to carry your own food and prepare it when you camp?

No problem. If you want a way to store food and be able to cook it, it can be done.

As a bare minimum, you'll need food storage containers (already covered in this book), along with a way to keep perishable food cool and a way to boil water or cook a meal.

As mentioned earlier, for storage of canned, bagged and non perishable food, I use a Ziploc Weather-shield storage tote – 15" wide by 19" deep by 11" high – which can be stored under the cot.

47

Clear plastic totes for storage

Almost any eleven inch tall plastic tote will work, but I prefer clear ones so I can see what is inside. Locking totes are more secure and in the case of food, will keep bugs out.

For storage of perishables and items that need to be kept cool, you'll want to use either a sturdy ice chest or a 12 volt cooler. If your budget will allow, consider getting a Yeti Roadie 20 cooler.

Yeti coolers have a well deserved reputation for keeping ice for up to five days and the Yeti Roadie 20 is the perfect size for your minivan.

The problem with the Yeti Roadie 20 (and all Yeti coolers) is they are quite expensive. The Roadie 20 runs about $250 from most retailers and there are rarely any discounts.

Still, if you can afford one and if keeping items cool for a number of days is important, consider a Yeti cooler.

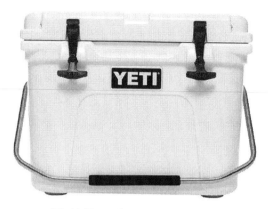

Yeti Roadie 20 Cooler

If a Yeti is not in your budget, there are a number of other well insulated coolers than can work.

Most inexpensive coolers will only keep ice for two to three days (depending on outside temperature), and none are suitable for storing food that must be kept frozen.

However, the low cost <u>Coleman 28 Quart Xtreme 3</u> cooler ($22.95 at Walmart) is one of the best, and in tests it was able to keep a fair amount of ice in the chest for three days.

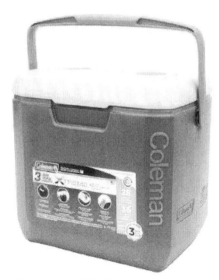

Coleman 28 Quart Xtreme 3

With any of these coolers, be prepared to buy ice often. This isn't a problem when you are traveling, but can be a pain if camped in a remote location.

Another option is to use a 12 volt cooler. While these won't freeze food, they can keep items cool for days – as long as the cooler is plugged into 12 volt power for at least ten hours each day.

I use a 12 volt cooler in my van and find it works almost as good as a Yeti Roadie 20, but at a fraction of the price. The model I have is a Koolatron P25 compact cooler. According to the manufacturer's website, it can keep food up to 40 degrees (F) cooler than the outside temperature.

Koolatron P25 12 volt cooler

If you do use a 12 volt cooler, you'll want to remember to unplug it from your car's 12 volt outlet at night so as not to drain the car's battery. If camping where electric hookups are available, you can use the Koolatron 110 volt AC adapter (sold separately), to power it without draining your battery.

If you do get the 110 volt adapter, it's a good idea to connect it to the Koolatron and let it cool down before leaving on your camping trip. Also consider putting a frozen blue ice pack in the bottom of the Koolatron to help keep items cooler longer.

The Koolatron P25 sells for around $70 and the newer P20 is $90. If you want to save money, check second hand stores and yard sales – you'll sometimes find used ones for around $20.00.

Koolatron P20

When I travel, I keep the Koolatron tucked in behind the passenger seat with the top facing the driver's seat. This makes it easy to reach in and get a cold drink while I drive.

Yard sales and second hand stores are also good places to look for used ice chests. Just make sure the ice chest isn't cracked and the drain spigot doesn't leak. (Don't pay more than five dollars for a used ice chest!)

To boil water and cook food, I use a single burner Coleman Butane Instastart Stove. It's small enough to fit in the bottom drawer of the cabinets I showed in a previous chapter and powerful enough to boil water in three minutes or less.

Coleman Instastart butane grill

For fuel, the stove uses a small butane canister that securely snaps into place. The canisters are safe for travel and can be found at Walmart and most camping stores for about $2.50. Each will give you about two hours of cooking.

Keep in mind that no matter what kind of grill you get, you should never use it inside you minivan. Having an open flame and cooking inside a van is not a good idea. Use a campground table or carry a small portable one with you and cook outside.

Along with the grill, you'll want a one quart sauce pan (to boil water and heat soup) and a small skillet. To make storing these items easier, look for camp cookware with removable handles. The MSR line up on Amazon or the camping section of Walmart will have what you need.

While shopping for your minivan kitchen, get a can opener, a cork screw, a metal spatula, a ladle and other kitchen gear you'll need for the meals you plan to prepare. You might also want to get a camp plate (Walmart or Dollar store) and silverware.

To clean pots and pans and dishes, carry a small sponge and a plastic bucket to use as your dish washing sink.

Lights, TV, and Fans

Since you'll be camping in your van after dark, you'll probably want a way to have lights, a fan, maybe even a TV. And even though your van probably has interior lights, you won't want to rely on these as they could possibly drain your van's starter battery.

A better choice is use a LED headlamp for reading or closeup work, LED flashlights when outside, and a UST Thirty Day LED lantern for interior light. These LED lights can operate for weeks on inexpensive batteries.

In my van, I carry <u>two glow in the dark LED flashlights</u> – so I can find them at night – a <u>Cree Ultrafire</u> for outside use, a <u>LED headlamp</u> for hands-free light, and a <u>UST thirty day LED lantern</u>.

The headlight and flashlights use AAA size batteries and I always carry a twelve pack of these with me.

The <u>30 Day lantern from Ultimate Survival Technologies</u> ($27 from Amazon), uses three 'C' cell batteries, and you can actually get 30 days of light before needing to replace them.

UST Thirty Day Lantern

In addition to LED lights, I pack a <u>Sony ICF-S10MK2 Pocket</u> AM/FM Radio ($19 at Amazon) so I can listen to local broadcasts without relying on the minivan battery. The Sony radio uses two AA batteries and can run for weeks without needing new ones.

I also carry an <u>Axess 7" LCD TV</u>, that can be powered by internal rechargeable batteries, car 12 volt or household 110 current. It comes with a remote, antenna and TV stand, and can receive over the air TV and play back video from a USB stick.

Axess 7" LCD TV with remote

I found the TV on <u>Amazon ($60)</u> and it lets me tune into local channels to watch news, weather and the major broadcast networks.

The included antenna is only good for pulling in nearby channels so I purchased a small amplified HD antenna to pull in more distant signals. When I camp, I set the HD antenna on the minivan's roof, run the cable through a window opening and connect it to the TV.

HD TV antenna (4" tall)

Having the ability to watch TV while camping might seem extravagant, but it's nice to be able to tune into the local channels and find out what's going on nearby.

I also carry a battery powered fan to create a breeze and a little white noise while I sleep. There are a number of fans that would work, but I chose a <u>Fan-tastic Endless Breeze 10"</u> fan, mainly because it uses less than a half an amp per hour on low speed.

Endless breeze 12 volt fan

The fan plugs into the 12 volt power port and will use less than 6 amp-hours overnight. If you have a 100-amp car battery, using the fan will barely make a dent in its charge.

But even though the fan doesn't use much power, I don't plug it or the TV or anything else into the minivan's power ports when the van is not running. Instead, I carry a portable power unit which produces 12 volt as well as 110 volt household current. A portable power unit like the one I have can supply power for hours and keep you from running down your van's battery.

Schumacher 1200 peak amp portable power

There are many different portable power units available with prices ranging from under $100 to well over $500. I found the one I have on sale at Woot for $62 with free shipping.

It has two twelve volt ports, two 110 ports, a USB recharger port, a built in air compressor (to air up flat tires), and built in powered jumper cables.

To power all these ports, the unit has an internal 22 amp-hour battery which can be recharged through either an 110 AC outlet or a 12 volt plug.

I find that I can plug in my Cool Breeze fan, the TV, and my phone and use them for several days before the power supply needs recharging.

When the charge display on the unit shows 30% or less, I'll camp where I can hook up to 110 household outlet and run an extension cord to the power supply to recharge it. It takes about 7 hours to get a full charge.

Because I do occasionally camp where electrical hookups are available, I carry a twenty five foot twelve gauge indoor/outdoor extension cord and a heavy duty power strip with multiple outlets.

I connect the extension cable to the external power source, plug in the power strip, and recharge my portable power supply as well as run the fan, TV and an electric heater (when needed).

Speaking of heat, when it comes to camping in very cold weather, my philosophy is, "if the weather is so cold that I need more heat in the van than having an extra blanket can provide, I will either go where the weather is warmer or camp where there are electrical hookups available."

I don't use and wouldn't recommend any kind of heater that has an open flame or produces fumes. No propane and kerosene heaters for me.

For the coldest nights, I carry and try to use a small ceramic electric heater plugged into external power.

If the weather is cold, campgrounds usually have lots of vacancies and it's a small price to pay to camp with electrical hookups if it means the difference between life and freezing to death.

When camping in your minivan, you can usually find a tent site with electric hookups for $15 a night or less. I've stayed in sites with electricity, wifi and access to hot and cold running water in the showers for $10 a night.

After a few days of traveling and camping in Walmart parking lots, it feels good to pull into a real campground and be able to recharge your batteries, run all your electrical appliances, take a shower and map out the road ahead.

Ready to go camping!

If you configure your minivan like I've shown in this book, you'll have a roadworthy camper with most of the amenities of a larger and much more expensive motorhome.

You'll be able to travel and camp in comfort and stay just about anywhere you choose. You can overnight in campgrounds, Walmart parking lots, at friend's homes, even curb-camp in full stealth mode.

You won't have to make any permanent changes to your minivan with the configuration I've shown and you won't need any special tools or carpentry skills.

With the items I've shown, you'll be able to convert your minivan into a camper in less than an hour, and convert it back to a daily driver just as quickly.

From the outside, it will look just like another run of the mill minivan. But on the inside, it'll be your comfortable, go anywhere, camping mobile on wheels.

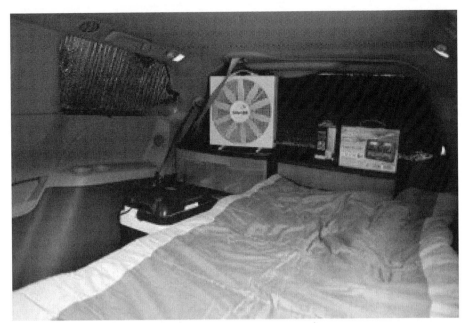

Ready to go camping!

In the above photo, you can see I've got a sleeping bag on the cot, a TV at the end of the bed, a fan on top of one of the storage units and the Koolatron cooler below the fan.

Not shown is the portable power unit which is tucked into the space between the storage unit on the right and the wall. It is positioned to be within reach of the power cords from the fan and the Koolatron cooler.

The top drawers of the storage unit are packed with clothes and bathroom items with heavier items packed in the bottom drawers.

Here's the view looking inside from the passenger sliding door.

View from passenger sliding door

You can see the water jug next to the Koolatron, with the power unit to the right of the jug. Just behind the power unit is the portable toilet – out of sight and packed away because it is rarely used.

The small box on top of the cabinet on the right at the foot of the bed contains the portable TV and antenna, both of which are usually packed away in the middle drawer of the storage unit.

As you can see, there is plenty of space to move around between the bed and the front seats. This makes it easy to find things and to pull out an under-bed storage tote to use as a computer or dining table.

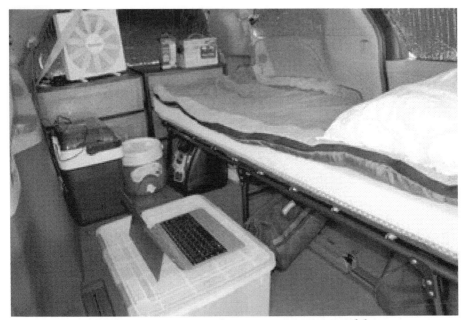

Storage tote used as a computer table

As mentioned in an earlier chapter, I keep my cameras, computer and tools in soft sided canvas tool bags. These are easy to pack into tight places and let you make use of all the cubby holes in the van.

You may have noticed that in converting my minivan into a mini-RV, I haven't done anything to use the front passenger seat as storage. You could certainly use it that way if you wanted to, but I prefer to keep that seat free.

That way, if I'm curb camping and don't have the window blinds up and someone looks inside the passenger window, they won't see anything that might suggest I'm camping in the van.

Of course, one of the advantages of outfitting your minivan is *you* get to decide what you want to put in it and where. The more you camp, the more you'll understand what you'll want in your van to make it a comfortable, safe and enjoyable experience.

Ready for a good night's sleep!

Where to Camp

One of the big advantages of camping in your mini-RV is you don't have to limit yourself to campgrounds and RV parks. You can pretty much camp just about anywhere you choose (within reason).

In a relatively new and clean minivan, you can park overnight in parking lots and curbside and not raise suspicion. Just make sure you aren't parked illegally or in a place that could be dangerous for you or oncoming traffic.

Look for level, well lit locations, out of the way of heavy traffic or early morning delivery trucks.

Park around other vehicles - never be the only vehicle on the street or in a lot. When it comes to overnight camping, there is safety and anonymity in numbers.

For maximum stealth, have your blackout curtains in place before you park. Keep light and sounds inside the van and don't give neighbors or those who pass by a reason to be suspicious.

Always lock your doors and don't sleep naked. If you have to make a hasty exit, it will go better if you are wearing clothes.

And avoid staying in one spot too long. Get there late in

the day, and leave early in the morning – unless camping in an authorized camping location.

Here are few places to consider when looking for a stealth camping spots.

- Walmart parking lots

- Loves Truck Stops

- Casino parking lots

- Hospital parking lots

- Truck Stops

- Car Dealerships

- Apartment complexes

- Fishing Piers

- Public boat ramp parking lots

- Small airport parking lots

- Strip shopping center parking

- Fairground parking lots

- State & county parks

- BLM land

- Rest areas (only if well lit)

- Cracker Barrel Restaurants, Dennys

- SmartPhone apps like WecampHere, Roadbreakers, AllStays Camp and RV to find free overnight parking. These apps show campgrounds as well as Walmarts and other plaees that don't restrict overnight parking.

Finding Free WiFi

If looking for free internet while on the road, try these places:

- MacDonalds and other fast food restaurants

- Panera Bread, Bob Evans

- Coffee Shops (Starbucks, etc)

- Malls

- Libraries

- Some truck stops

- State Welcome Centers (Florida)

- If you carry a smartphone, you can use the PDAnet app to tether your phone to your computer to get reletively fast internet on the computer. This is what I use this when I need to update my website from my laptop computer while on the road.

- WeFi Pro – app shows public wifi around you (free)

Note: There is always a risk when using public wifi, so avoid entering private or credit card information or entering login details at bank and financial websites. Assume everything you do when using public wifi is visible to others.

A few extras to carry along

In addition to everything mentioned so far, here are a few extras I carry with me in the minivan.

- **8' X 10' tarp** – it can be used to create an awning shade by tying off to roof racks

- **100 feet of 3/16 inch cotton clothesline** – to tie off tarp - $5.95 at Walmart, Amazon

- **Kidde Automotive Fire Extinguisher** – Walmart $10.31

- **Garmin 6" GPS** – So I don't get too lost – Woot/Amazon ($88 refurbished)

- **G1WC dash-cam** – to record on video everything that happens on the road – Amazon ($48)

- **First Aid kit** – just in case

- **Extra Batteries** – AA, AAA, C

- **Duct Tape**

- **Scissors** – to open plastic packages

- **Utility Knife**

- **Trash Bags**

- **Zip Lock Bags**

- **Cotton Gloves**

- **Tire Air pressure gauge**

- **Carbon Monoxide alarm**

- **Purell Hand Sanitizer**

- **Extra pair of sun glasses and reading glasses**

- **Smart phone Apps –**

  - RV Parky

  - We Camp Here

  - All Stays Camp and RV

  - Around Me

  - Roadbreakers

  - Field Trip

  - Raindar

  - PDANet

  - WeFi Pro

List of camping gear mentioned in this book

Here is a complete list of every item mentioned in this book, along with the source for the item and approximate price paid.

- **Reflectix 24-in x 25-ft Reflective Roll Insulation** – available at Lowes ($23.95), Amazon, Walmart online

- **Intro-Tech Automotive Windshield Sun Shade** – custom windshield sun shade for your mini-van (appr $30) – Autoanything.com, Amazon.com

- **AVS Window Vent Visors** – Autoanything.com, Amazon.com, local auto parts stores ($40 - $60)

- **Coleman Ridgeline III Camp Bed Folding Camping Cot** – Walmart online ($53.00), Amazon, eBay

- **3" Twin size 5.5 memory foam mattress pad** – eBay ($53.00)

- **Male and Female 'Pee' bottle** – Amazon, eBay ($4.00) – or go to the local Dollar store and get a plastic juice pitcher ($1.00)

- **Century 6205 2.6 gallon portable toilet** – Amazon $78.89

- **Reliance Bio-Blue Toilet Deodoran**t 12 pack – Amazon ($6.99)

- **Coleman Party Stacker 2 Beverage Cooler** – Walmart online ($10.94), Amazon

- **Sterlite Three Drawer Rolling Carts** (2) – Walmart, $17.88

- **Coleman 28 Quart Xtreme Cooler** – Walmart ($22.95)

- **Koolatron P25 12 volt cooler** – Amazon ($70.99)

- **Coleman Butane Instastart Stove** – Amazon, Walmart ($21.72)

- **Butane Fuel Canisters** – Walmart $2.97

- **Camping Cookware** – Small boiler and skillet. Apprx $20.

- **UST Thirty Day Lantern** – Amazon ($27)

- **Sony ICF-S10MK2 Pocket AM/FM Radio** - Amazon ($18.99)

- **Axess 7-Inch LCD TV** w/rechargeable battery, stand and USB inputs – Amazon ($57)

- **Fan-tastic Endless Breeze 10" fan** – Amazon ($55.00). Other less expensive and smaller fans would work just as well, including the 02 Cool 5" fans that are under $10.

- **Schumacher 1200 Peak Amp Portable Power** – Available at Amazon, Walmart, Lowes. Retail $120. Found at Woot.com for $62.

Budget Build

Clearly, you don't need every item I've shown in this book to create a cozy minivan camper. If you're on a budget and want to keep spending to minimum, here are the things I'd suggest you get.

- Reflectix window treatments - $24

- AVS Vent visors - $50

- Coleman Camp Bed - $50

- Pee Bottle - $1 (from the dollar store)

- Plastic bucket for makeshift toilet ($1)

- Coleman Stacker II water jug - $12

- Coleman 28 qt Xtreme 3 Ice Chest - $24

- Coleman Instastart Butane stove - $20

- Sterlite 3 drawer storage cabinets ($15)

You should be able to get all the above for under $200. If you search yard sales and second hand stores, you might be able to get everything for under a hundred.

Add some cooking gear, flashlights, a first aid kit and a sleeping bag and you'll be ready to hit the road.

Enjoy the adventure

When you have your minivan set up as a comfortable camper, you can enjoy the adventure of traveling across the country and experiencing life on the road.

You'll discover new places, meet new friends, and create memories that you'll cherish forever.

You might even write about a book about your experiences. So be sure to take a camera so you can share with others all the interesting things you see along the way.

For the most part, camping in your minivanRV will be a safe and pleasurable experience. However, you do have to be careful when choosing a spot to spend the night.

Avoid high crime areas and try to park in well lit places where others are parked nearby.

Do that and you'll live to see another day.

Whatever you do, be sure and enjoy the adventure!

The adventure continues . . .

If you liked this book, please post a positive review on Amazon. Also take a look at my other books, including:

<u>Buying a used motorhome without getting burned</u>

<u>Mango Bob</u> – Motorhome adventure

<u>Mango Lucky</u> - Motorhome adventure

<u>Mango Bay</u> - Motorhome adventure

<u>Mango Glades</u> - Motorhome adventure

<u>Mango Key</u> - Motorhome adventure

   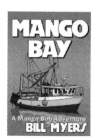

Printed in Great Britain
by Amazon

49459561R00047